# Confessions of a Young Poet

## J Nicole

## *From My Heart to Yours*

First and foremost, I would like to thank God for His many blessings, for blessing me with the gift of writing, the ability to place emotions on a page, and placing words in my heart to write. To my wonderful, amazing, and loving husband, Thadd, thank you for pushing me to see the potential in my writing, for reminding me constantly that my dreams are too important to push aside, and for loving me through it all. I love you infinitely. To my loving parents, Leon and Erica, thank you for the years of love and support. It has never gone unnoticed, and I am forever grateful. To my sister, Jada, and my brother, Leon, Jr., **WE MADE IT!** To everyone who has in some way been part of this journey, **THANK YOU.** Honestly, it's too many of you to name, and I don't want to miss anyone.

At the heart of this collection of poetry is my relationship with God. Every test, every trial, every triumph, and every whispered prayer finds its place here. I wanted to offer a collection that honors the authenticity of life, from the tender moments of joy to the quiet battles fought in the shadows of our minds. I hope that these poems will speak to a wide audience: those who know Christ and those who are still searching for Him.

Whether you find yourself resonating with the longing for healing, the pursuit of identity, or the celebration of love, my prayer is that these pages offer you a place of connection and reflection. A place where you can hide yourself for a few moments, knowing that Christ can still find you.

For those who share my faith, you will see the fingerprints of Christ throughout this work. His love is the thread that holds it all together, the reason I can share even the rawest parts of my story with confidence. For those who do not yet know Him, I invite you to journey through these poems with an open heart. My hope is not to preach but to offer—to offer a glimpse of the grace that has carried me.

This is not a collection that shies away from sensitive topics. Life is complex, and these poems reflect that complexity. Yet, in every piece, there is a thread of hope, a light that guides the way. I want these poems to speak truth in love, to encourage dialogue, and to remind every reader that they are not alone.

Thank you for taking the time to read this collection. I pray that as you turn each page, you are reminded of the beauty and purpose in your own story. As long as you have breath – you still have purpose.


All my love,

*J Nicole*

*For my angels,*

*Mary A. Whipps (1936 – 2010)*

*Beulah Taylor (1922 – 2017)*

*Rufus Whipps (1936 – 2019)*

*Frank Hartwell (1945 – 2019)*

*Barbara Taylor (1947 – 2021)*

*Your prayers are the reason I'm still standing.*


*For my first-born son,*

*Jeremiah Eion Macklin*

*May you forever know that dreams are __POSSIBLE__*

# Notice ME!

The face of an angel,

Your smile contains amazing

Your speech is comparable

To a heavenly choir singing 'Glory in the Highest'

Yet I'm unnoticeable to you

Your glance causes me

To go into a neurological shock

I freeze instantly

Falling into the hypnosis of your beauty

Such things should be a crime

And if you would notice me

I'd willingly be your jailer

Only imprisoning you

With abundant love

Hugs and kisses consistently

Support unfailing

Notice me,

Let me consume your thoughts

Causing you to crave midnight

Only for me to invade the empty spaces of your soul

If only for those few minutes

Just so you can see me

You don't know me

I don't stand out like they do

You can't tell that my heart stops

My lungs cease from accepting oxygen

Permitting my brain only to depict a movie of us

# Love Doesn't Live Here Yet

I never intended to love you,

But between midnight and dawn

I had fallen for your type

It's impossible for amazing to be wrapped in one's kiss

And love being visible in one's eyes

But just as I peered into what seemed to be your soul,

I envisioned that love could indeed be true

And you cared not

That his name was written in the sands of time

Between the meeting of my thighs

That another had tattoo his name upon my heart

Although I had tried to remove it,

It left scars

You began to repair the brokenness of my soul

Singing sweet lullabies, maybe lies

That told of a prince charming, knight in shining armor,

Waiting to rescue this damsel in distress

Trying to escape the dragon's harmful caress

I never intended to love you,

But you seemed to have the moon's illumination

Wrapped into your smile

And a 1920s gangster swagger

Wrapped into your style

You were a smooth criminal,

Stealing my heart before I had a chance to put up my guard

You frightened me,

Showering me with gifts that did not include a baggage fee

You lifted the bags off my shoulders,

And carried them for me,

Claiming that I was no longer able to carry them

As though they were not part of my apparel

Before you appeared on this Polaroid

But you said "Bag lady, you gone hurt yo' back running around
like that"

So I allowed you to share the burden

Of a childhood been stripped

From a young girl who had no idea

That love didn't mean feeling as though

Someone has stabbed you in the heart and back

A young girl who didn't know

That the most beautiful person,

Stared her in the face each morning

And I told myself that I would not catch "hero syndrome"

I never intended to love you,

Yet that winged cherub decided to shoot his arrow,

Into the depths of my heart

And claim it as yours

# Upendo (Love)

Rain and tears

Drenched the golden-brown complexion

Once an acrylic painting,

Transformed into a watercolor masterpiece

He was frozen

In a trance

Holding a golden band

That once sealed his destiny with her

*Nakupenda*[1]

He whispered breathlessly

Only audible to God and himself

Praying she would return

An archangel causing grief

To his love-damaged heart

*Upendo*[2]

A word he once understood,

That backfired quickly

As an old model Lincoln would,

He didn't understand

How a woman could be so vindictive

And lash out because of her past,

*Upendo*

[1] Nakupenda – Swahili for "I love you"

[2] Upendo – Swahili for "love"

# Midnight to a Golden End

Lying here,

Hoping when midnight

Turns to a golden end

That within your arms

I'll remain

Faithful I am

To the belief that you will stay

Like a saint believing in heaven

Yet my mind says it's a lie

A lie,

That I allowed

To become my fantasy,

Pleasuring my inner thoughts

To become the thing I cherished most

The happiness I coveted from others

I need not your memories

When your presence is requested

Lying here,

Watching midnight

Slightly end in gold

The rising and falling of your chest

My lullaby,

Slowly rocking me back to sleep

Peacefully I smile,

Yet when I awake I'm holding myself

# Love Letters

Coded messages

Hearts and arrows

Spread across blue and white fields

Looking as though small children

Had decided to write valentines

To winter crushes on a steaming summer's day

Your name

Written in elegant letters

The penmanship of trembling hands

The beginning, middle, and end

All begin,

"I love you..."

Words I dare not utter too loudly,

For fear of their power and virtue

For fear of my comprehension of them

The hearts continue to flutter through the page

As my heart skips a beat with each word

Each sentence,

Holding truth and beauty

As new as each spring

Only to show you

That I feel for you.

# Let Me In

I know where your hat lies,

There is your temporary home

You put it down

Stay awhile

Until a different wind decides to blow

Sending you to the next "home"

Next pretty face with a slim waist

But where does your lonely heart reside

Is it locked away in the deepest part of your soul?

Crying for something secure

Instead of late-night rendezvouses

Can my hands be the home it's looking for?

There's plenty room

My heart, your only company

Because it's lonely too

But if they reside together

I promise I'll play fair

No home court advantage

The playing field is even

Give up your roaming baby

The days of being a barbarian are over

True love awaits

A love like Paris and Helena

I know you think this is just a sweet talking game

But I won't put your feelings to shame

# Could You Let Me Love You?

Let go of your apprehensions,

If only for a few moments,

Open your yearning ears and your mending heart

And listen to this message from my soul to yours

Relax yourself,

And fall into the embrace of arms,

Strong enough to help you carry your burdens,

So heavy on your crumbling spine

Arms capable of sustaining you when you begin to fall,

In love with me,

That ground is cold and hard,

And while you know all too well the feeling,

You will never have to feel it again as long as you're with me

Let's take a walk on the other side of Lover's Land,

When the weather is less tumultuous

And your heart is mended by

My willingness to wait

Patience is key

And I'd rather not have you chasing,

Yesteryear again,

That crazy grouchy female

That has your heart in shambles,

When it should have a strong heartbeat for

Someone like me,

See, it's crazy,

But I can tell you that your future is brighter than your past and present,

If you take a chance on someone

Who knows what it feels like,

To be left on that cold hard ground

And to find yourself left to bear pain

That shouldn't be yours to begin with

Open your heart and,

Let me in

# I'm Not Her

I'm not her,

The girl that left your mahogany cheeks

Soaked with tears

And your heart feeling as though it had traveled the streets of New York

I want to mend the hurt,

But I can't if you're not willing to look past it.

Tell me, you're willing to give love a chance again.

I'm not her,

The girl who passed you in the crowd

Who you gave all your love to

And she never gave you the satisfaction of a simple greeting

I love you for you

Your flaws are a handsome part of you.

But you can only see those things

That she seemed to like

And imagine I'm like that too.

I'm not her,

She left you out in the rain

Like a sad puppy on a warm summer's evening

I brought you in from the rain

Cleaned you up

And gave you a new place to stay,

Yet you feel as though you owe me

And that's not the case

I'm not her

My feelings run deeper than the surface

Because your physical appearance doesn't matter to me

And I could care less whether you're broke or rich

Whether you're in school or working

I'm not her

Worrying about how society sees us

I'd just rather be with someone

Who loves me for me too,

But until you see

That I'm not her

This relationship will stay,

In the same place

And never go anywhere.

Baby I wanna hear wedding bells

Carry your namesake

Grow old together

And spend eternity together

But I'm not her

And that's what you can't see.

The hurt you're holding on to

Has left you insecure

And with that, I can't deal

I'd rather leave you alone

Then let your fears linger on

I'm not her...

# Delusional

IVs through my veins,

"Cardiac arrest"

The doctors say

Scrambling to find a cure,

They don't know

A broken heart,

Could cause Goliath to fall

Cancer spreading

Can't find the source

If they can catch up to you,

They'll find the cause and the cure

Of how someone so strong,

Could end up falling to their knees

You've done to me,

What Delilah did to Samson

You were the needle

That feeds my addiction

Love,

I couldn't afford to keep up my habit

Lying to myself

Saying it will all be okay

A broken heart

Will cause the sanest person

To become delusional

# A Letter to My Ex-Lover

Dear ex-lover

Glimmering cards and letters,

Adorn my scrapbook of memories

Most of them from you

Polaroids shouldn't make me

Long for your touch as much

Yet staring at the plastic image of you,

Has me feeling,

Like an addict,

Opting that her last dollar is worth drugs

I needed you to breathe

And since you departed

My breathing hasn't been the same

Dear ex-lover,

When my daughter asks,

"What does it feel like to be in love?"

I'll describe our first kiss,

Sweet, a taste that lingers

Like honey, bittersweet

And when she comes

Eyes full of cold, icy tears

I'll tell her,

That falling out of love isn't easy

Knowing that I'm still in love with you

Dear ex-lover,

Do you know what the tears of an angel look like?

Ice crystals,

Spread across the soft warm earth,

Lingering only for seconds

Only to disappear as quietly as they've appeared

Dear ex-lover,

I hate to pour my heart

Into a page-long poem

And bare my soul for strangers,

But poetry is truth, right?

# You Love Me Not

Your love has captured me

A concentration camp

Without a release date

Only option is to break-free

But like heroin to a drug addict

I can't leave you alone

Baby, I can't stop cold turkey

You have to wean me off this

Your love has a hold on me

A chain around my fragile heart

Squeezing firmly

You promised not to break it

Yet renovations must be made dear

I can either escape

Or die trying

The hold you have on me is deadly

Like a copperhead's bite

Poison, destroying me slowly

And shaking you off

Isn't as simple as it seems

Like going from elementary math

To college algebra

It requires a level of skill and causes difficulties

You have cut me deeper

Than any surgeon's incision will

Cutting directly to my soul

Singing a siren's song, causing me to be lost from home

Baby you used to love me

Or was it a figment of my imagination

How could you hurt me?

Yet, I won't leave.

# Love Rant I

The memories of yesteryear,

Seems to hold me hostage

I am placed in a chokehold

By words and laughter

Laughter, which haunts me

On sunny days, when the air is crisp

When the basketball court is empty

And I'm alone shooting threes

You were my opponent

But you forfeited a championship game

Due to fear and intimidation

"Baby, let the memories go..."

My conscience coaxes my heart

To release my biggest roadblock

My destination is him

The newest guy

But I can't get to him

Due to my leftover love for you

Baby, leftovers are no good

When they are cold and months old

It's causing me to be sick

The memories of yesteryear

Holding me hostage

But my mind has a machete

Ready to cut you

# Love Rant II

A hostage of words left unspoken

And a cold heart

Both detrimental to the person

I am becoming

Causing my addiction of you

To slowly creep into my veins again

Old habits die hard

And they do die slowly

As slowly as the tears fall against my earthen cheeks

I remind myself that rain,

Doesn't always stay

Baby tell me

Did you ever really love me?

Not the "me" I claimed to be

But the real me

Tell me that this leftover infatuation

Will make a perfect meal

Play master chef in my heart

And plan our anniversary dinner

A dinner worth staying for

Worth the heat of the flames

No, I don't want you back

And I'll never reopen for business

Permanent shut-down

Renovations will be made,

But there's a new chef in town.

# My Morning (Fantasizing of You)

Lying in a bed,

Watching the sun kill the stars' light

I wonder if the dawn will bring you home

If morning will bring a brighter beginning

My sleep was interrupted by dreams of you

Creeping up on me and startling my spirit

My heart raced,

And I awoke reaching for you,

Knowing you won't return anytime soon

How could you break me down like a Lego Masterpiece?

Leaving me broken and crying wolf to the next woman

When it is you who left me in a sandbox for the other boys to find

Mama told me not to run to you

That your heart was like snow, so cold

But I needed your company

Now I'm painting a fantasy of morning

Where the rising and falling of your chest

Is a sweet lullaby keeping me asleep.

Can you let go so easily?

Or will you carry the hurt as I am?

You're off being a rolling stone

And I'm stuck in a zone

A trance of brokenness

Bring back my morning

And heal my broken heart

Hold it in your hands.

Be the potter…

Just promise…

You won't drop me

# The Break-Up

The words you said,

Never clearly registered in my head

They never reached the full potential of understanding

Yet, they reached my memory bank in an instant

And replayed as though a record had skipped

They were clearly stated

Over a glass of Möet and Chardonnay

That she was your fiancée, and you had to let me go

"Let go me…"

An affair that lasted over two years

But you had to let…me…go…

The words left your lips as chocolate

Smooth and sweet,

As though the transition would be as easy

I sat back and took in the scenery around me

A five-star Italian restaurant

Pure white tablecloths

Fine china and wine bottles seemed inviting each time

A fine establishment

Owned by some old mob boss who couldn't drop the game

Yet ironically you were here dropping me like an old habit

Is it that easy?

To let go of a love you've known since high school

Like Donnell Jones, you claimed it was unfair

Yet you left anyhow

Paid the bill and said you'll see me at the wedding

And I just smiled,

Nodded my head and continued to sip the wine

You let go,

But I could never move on so easily.

# Separation

There were no warning sirens,

Nothing that could prepare his heart,

For the train wreck that was in sight.

A whirlwind that came and destroyed the house

He so desperately tried to build.

She wanted out,

She wanted to give up,

Happiness no longer dwelling within their four walls,

She wanted more than he could give,

Wanted her cake and eat it too,

She needed to see what the world had to offer.

It hit him as though a ton of bricks,

Had fallen on his once strong heart,

Golden band on ring finger seemed to melt

And he could do nothing about it

Love wouldn't make her stay,

After all those years,

Love wasn't even present anymore.

His heart was now as paper,

She had complete control

Tossing it to and fro

She couldn't make up her mind

And he didn't force her to

There were no warning sirens

Leading to their relationship ending in flames,

No hero to rescue him

And no firefighters to extinguish the flames

They were heading for train wreck

Divorce,

But she already had a safety net close by

# Late Night Sippin'

The sound of raindrops,

Against my windowpane

The fireplace burning bright

Reminds me of the flames

Ignited in my heart for you

Yet like these flames

You're untouchable

A star out of my reach

That I continue to wish upon

Praying, maybe, just maybe

I'll hear your footsteps

Come through the door

Feel the outline of your triceps and biceps

Embrace my petite frame

And put my doubts and fears to shame

No tears tonight,

Or silent cries

Just a glass of my favorite red wine

And the sound of this pen

Hitting the page

Only the staining of the ink

Will show how my heart bleeds

And how I overthink

The reason you left me

I envy her

And the life you've now created apart from me

I sit wishing I was yours

While you cater to her

Nothing to do,

But sip this wine

Until my eyes are no longer wet

With tears of yesteryear and regrets

# Soldier Gone AWOL

You disappear for days at a time

A soldier gone AWOL

My heart won't have you court-martialed

You pled not guilty by reason of insanity

Insanity…

Doing the same thing repeatedly

And expecting the same result

My heart won't shut you out

Yet you come and go as you please

Telling me you have a mission

A mission?

Is not my heart the land you're trying to conquer?

Like Erykah,

I cried for you, painted blue for you,

Hated for you, and hated you too,

Just to show you I was down for you,

But what you do?

Run off with the girl who gave you the best view

And I knew it was true,

But my heart wouldn't let me lose you

Thought I needed a boo

A guy that didn't understand

That love is only made perfect by God

Temporary happiness fulfilling the void I had inside

I never knew joy

And I thought you could,

And I wish you would have

But dreams don't always come true

Or do they?

Sweetheart, I'm too in love with you

And I turned all those other guys down

Just so I could keep you around

I'm on a merry-go-round

Of emotions with you

I miss you,

But it's time to let you go.

# Nothing Is the Same

Imagine

A lyricist with no words

A poet with no rhymes

A beach with no sand

A clock with no time

They say all wounds heal over time

But I swear a week

Has felt like months on end.

And it's crazy

I said I would never get hurt

Kept a ten-foot wall around my heart

Just to let you come through the front gate

And I tried not to depend on hearing your voice

Before I fell asleep at night

And I tried not to imagine

Your arms wrapped tightly around my waist

After we would play around like little children

We were day and night

Guess opposites do attract

But even the strongest bonds wax old

I saw my world through your eyes

But it all started to fade

I got tired of the lies

And I got tired of crying

Falling asleep wondering if I was right

And it's crazy, I tried

To hold on to something

That was never meant to be

Silly me

For dreaming of the greatest possible thing:

Sharing my life with someone who cared

But maybe it was a fallacy

A beautiful nightmare

I never wanted to awake

But the awakening was rude

And what you said was cruel

Yet I still want to cling to you

Like a child to his mother's bosom

Mama said, "You chose him."

Wish I had checked the other choices

Thought if I had what everyone else did

I'd be happy

But it made me miserable still

Guess I gotta swallow that pill,

My mind telling me to chill,

But my heart is far from calm,

Reminding me of a storm on the gulf,

I called your bluff,

And now you're looking

As though your world has ended

It's crazy

I'm tired of this,

Never been so tired in my life

Nothing is the same...

# Breaking Down

She conjured enough strength

To dam rivers from flowing

Her mahogany cheeks held a smile

Reflecting a waning crescent moon

(He left too soon.)

Ripped and mangled

Her heart crawled in a corner

Cried for sudden death

(He just left.)

*Upendo* and *nakupenda*

Were mere fragments of memories,

It's difficult to tell the difference between,

Falling for the right one and loving the wrong king

Royalty was far from his nature

Who would leave stranded his subjects

Let alone his Nubian queen

Queens show no emotions

That's what was taught in the beginning

But his rejection caused the Nile to flow

From light brown eyes

Reflecting Cleopatra's

Flowing down her mahogany cheeks

# Lover to Lover

Dear lover,

Touch me as it were our first time,

I am Helen of Troy

You are a dedicated gladiator

Risking your life, just for me

Utilize your wooden horse strategy

To capture me

Dear lover,

Kiss me as sweetly as we first did

Make me experience I am the Juliet, to you, my Romeo

Our families forbid our romance

But like a fat kid to *Hershey's*

I can't resist

Dear lover,

Date me as if you dread losing me,

I am a rare gem

Priceless,

Highly esteemed,

You have the golden key,

To a heart newly renovated

Dear lover

I refuse to stay

If you can't treat me,

As if I'm your future queen

If you can't show me

I am your Aphrodite

Dear lover,

Love me,

Like you're afraid to leave

Like you're afraid to see me walk away

# First Romance

My first love's touch,

Felt as if,

God himself molded his hands,

To fit my waist perfectly

His kiss sweeter than honey

Lips perfect against mines

He held my heart

A newly renovated space

With more than enough room,

To allow him to dwell in it

My first love

Knew exactly what to say,

Like a mother's words

To a discouraged child,

He would whisper in my ear

Just how much I meant to him

How much he needed me,

I made him complete

My first love

Completed me

# Fireflies, Butterflies, & Clouds

Memories dance within the four corners of my mind

As fireflies on a warm summer night

I try to bottle them within my empty heart

And observe them illuminate the vision of my future

A future with you,

In this unforetold sojourn, we call life

All thoughts seem to swarm around being your wife

Your name is stated

And the butterflies swarm my stomach,

Tell me,

Can you feel them too?

The butterflies and fireflies

Whenever I'm around

That makes you feel as though,

Your feet have been lifted off the ground

Take flight love

Because you have me floating on a cloud

# Limitless Love (Distance)

(Distance)

A word that reflects no thought

Only numbers,

Miles

Inches

Hours

Minutes

Seconds

(Distance)

As far as the eye can see

As long as a train will ride

As far as a plane will fly

(Distance)

Love has no odometer

No mileage per gallon

No baggage fee required

Love travels farther than any car

Faster than any plane

Smoother than train

(Distance)

Numbers that are void

When love is involved

# A Passionate Dance

His eyes

The color of nutmeg

Her lips

As soft as rose petals kissed by morning dew

The softness of her lips against his

Could send him into a place he couldn't describe

They were emotionally, mentally, and sexually attracted

So, tonight was the night

They started the waltz

Strutting a mean tango

Salsa their way to an intimate moment

But always cha-cha around it

Trying to avoid missing a step

They connected perfectly

Nutmeg

Soft rose petals

Meeting simultaneously, explosively, enchantingly

Slowly

His movements matched hers

Their pulses creating a rhythm

Their shallow breathing, the tempo

Turning their fast-paced dance

Into a last call slow dance

Turning their love

Into a late night, early morning passion

# Love Lockdown

The look in your eyes

Was a magnetic force

That pulled my waiting lips to yours

A bed of crushed rose petals

I quivered

A slight arctic breeze

Surged through my bones

Caused my heart to run,

A 100-meter dash

Jump over my fears

And fall into your waiting, empty hands

What is this confinement you have me in?

I want a lifetime sentence

Lock me away in love

And throw away the key

I deserve this

Believe me

Because my heart

Is Rome in ruins

A once beautiful city

Destroyed by war

It has such a beautiful history

But too many battle wounds,

Scars that you find beautiful

So I'm beautifully flawed

The love oozing from you

Is giving me a contact high

And I can't contain my laughter and joy

I have the munchies for your love

So feed me this manna of love

That indisputably has given me life

Joy at its best

# He Took Me

His hands felt like crushed rose petals,

Against my delicate skin

A man's hands shouldn't feel as soft as his

Something this pleasing should be sin

Shooting a wave of apprehension up my spine

Causing my knees to buckle

And the walls around my heart,

To come tumbling as if they surrounded Jericho

This 'Joshua' was dedicated

To see past the ruins of Rome,

The scars left by civil wars

The ugliness I've tried to hide from the world

He uncovered them as if they were buried treasure,

Yes, captain saw pass the meeting of my thighs

He made love to my mind

Reciting lines as though he was Othello

And I, his Desdemona

Painted a picture like Da Vinci,

And made this Mona Lisa smile

My guard fell as though the Berlin wall,

But the vulnerability did not scare me

I wanted to be the Cleopatra to this Antony

His beautiful wife to be

Rings intertwining

A fire and desire that cannot be contained

Someone call 911, my heart has caught flame

Firemen cannot contain the blaze

His love is a torch that lights the way

Pass every relationship that went wrong

Rebuilding a bridge back to lover's land

Hand and hand, I'll continue to stand

By his side until the world ends

And an eternity after that

# I'll Love You

You should know,

That 'through thick and thin'

Is not a proper term, in our relationship,

And neither is 'for better or worse'

But rather

I'll love you

Even on your bad days

When you think not to call

Or even utter the words "I love you"

Allowing me not to rest so easily at night

Or I'll love you

Even if you catch a bad attitude

Over an opinion I've stated.

I'll love you,

On your best days

When you light up my world,

With a gentle kiss and smile

Or give me roses just because I'm yours

And I'll love you

When you hold me tightly during a thunderstorm

Knowing that you'll never let go

And that the rising and falling of your chest is my sweet lullaby

I'll love you

When the sun shines

And when the rain pours

Because some people will leave when things get tough

But with you, I'll forever stay.

# I Never Wanted Love

I allowed the beat of his heart

Become the tempo of my heart's content

His strong arms foreshadowed

The grip he would have on my heart

A firm, yet gentle grip

That frightened me

Because a grip of such caliber

Can cause hysteria

At the thought of it being loosened

The first thing that came to mind

Was to tell you

"I love you…"

Not because I felt it

Just seemed it was right to say

Yet the more times stated

The easier to believe

Yea, I believed

It's not easy loving you

Because the time I needed

You couldn't always give

And I dealt with it, if only for a season

Time can do crazy things to your mind

Delusion sets in

Can't really explain it

Love was in the air

And I caught it like a common cold

I thought I had let you go

But the mere sound of the first syllable of your name

Sends my heart into oblivion

I never wanted to fall in love

It happened unknowingly

Against my will

# Never Ending Romance

These days it's never goodnight,

But merely never-ending conversations

Spilling over into the morning hours

The smell of coffee at dawn

I'm addicted to the scent of your cologne

And it lingers on my favorite t-shirt of yours

Sitting in the very place you left it

Across our king-sized bed

We still act as though we're teenagers

Having a secret love affair

Scared my father will pick up the phone and end

The snickering coming from both of us

Puppy love

And I never say goodnight,

But kiss you gently on the lips

Before being lulled to sleep by the melody of your chest

You leave me weak

Like I've been dehydrated of love

I thirst for you

But not like these young girls do

See my thirst is quite different

And can't be quenched with lies and sold-out dreams

I don't seek fallacies

I never believed fairy tales

Yet, I believe I am your queen

And you are my king

I am your Eve

And you are my Adam,

I was taken from your ribs

Lost at birth to be found again

And I won't be Delilah, Samson

I won't dare take your strengths away

Because they keep me safe

When all my strength to fight has left me

And I'll be the wife you will love,

Just as Proverbs 31

And I'll love you, my husband

As long as God is the foundation of our home

As long as God remains our centerpiece

We'll never have to worry if we're meant to be

# Letter to My Unborn (Confessions of a Young Mother)

You are a part of me

And the inevitable decision

To bring you into this world

Was not up for discussion

Neither was it the choice made by your father

But I chose to bring life unto you

Because I know you'll cast light

Into this shadowy life of mines

You give me joy

Although your smile I have yet to see

And you will be great

Don't worry about being loved

Because I love you from the depths of my soul

And that's deep

You're a consequence of seconds of pleasure

A blessing in disguise to my torn life

I never knew what a family looked like

But you will know what it means to have a family

A host of aunties and uncles

My sweet baby

You are my joy

You weren't planned,

But you won't be avoided

Because you need love too

Just as I did when your father planted you

And I'll watch you mature and grow

And hope you make better decisions

Don't let the world turn you

Into a statistic

You're more than that

You're the next president

The next Nobel Peace Prize recipient

The next Olympic gold medalist

But even if you want

To be the next teacher of the year

Mommy will always support you

For you are a part of me

And the inevitable decision to love you

Was never up for discussion

You have brought joy to my life

Although your smile, I have yet to see

# Cries of the Amistad

Taken from their motherland,

Ankles and wrists chained,

A three-ring circus act,

And they were the opener

Cast into shark infested waters,

Turned into breakfast, lunch, and supper

If their performance did not please the audience

Speaking their native language

Bantu, Swahili

Longing to be heard, understood

"Give us free."

Not a statement,

But a fragment of command,

Demanding the rights promised to them by God alone

"Give us free."

The ship in turmoil,

Captives loosened of their bonding ties

Placing a vengeful death upon those that deprived them,

Of their native land, language, name, and pride

Exported them thousands of miles away

Only for them to play hide and seek with sharks

Have their flesh ripped from their bodies by the forceful blows of whips

Babies stripped from their wombs,

Future princes and princesses

Revolt and death are their only freedom,

Revolt the only option

Chains now gone,

Captors, now captives

Freedom granted

# Where Do the Weary Stand?

These tears I've cried

Have become pillows

Cushioning my weary eyes

Causing my soul to collapse

And my spirit to willingly die

Just for a chance to rest

I yearn for the joy

That others seem to experience

To kill the stress

That seems to boggle my mind

That causes my limbs to shut down

To the form of cooked spaghetti

Numb to pain and easily broken

My heart creeps into a black hole and weeps

Of pain and insecurities

It longs to forget and regrets

They say,

"There is no rest for the weary,"

Yet,

Where do they journey

When the road less traveled

Turns rocky

Their feet can no longer tread the path

Their burdens heavy

On their necks the yoke of life

And their spine subject to break,

At any given moment

Where do the weary stand?

# Insecurity (These Tears)

These tears I've cried

Sitting beside me in buckets of shame

Have become my drinking water

Replenishing wetness to my throat

Suppressing screams of the monster within me

Insecurity, that monster hidden

Within my closet full of skeletons

Showing itself in broad daylight

Instead of staying in my darkest nights

He said, "You look like Miss Piggy"

She said, "I could have your man"

Statements that made me feel four inches tall,

And pray that invisibility was a superpower bestowed on me

These tears I've cried

Have turned into a raging river

Swiftly carrying pain and disappointment

Right down to the ocean of my soul

Reminding my eyes just why they were waterfalls in the first place

More like Niagara Falls

Dumping water onto the craters below my tired eyes

Craters dug deep by restless and sleepless nights

Wrestling with secrets and lies in my sleep

And fighting insecurity in daytime heat

These tears are my drinking water

Yet, I'm drowning

# Black History 365

Stolen from our mother's breast

Forced to settle in a foreign land

Artistic carvings sketched across our backs

Painted in red, black, and blue

Stripped of our native language, name, very being

Savages! Animals! Inferior!

All thoughts etched into our virgin minds

Yessir, Nahsir, no freedom in sight

400 years later the chains are dropped from our hands and feet

And placed on our already brainwashed minds

Forced to think this was a way of life

Separate but equal, Plessy v. Ferguson 1896

But why did we have to enter the back door

If the front is much closer

All men are created equal?

Apparently not true

One man had a dream it could be so

Marched to let the world know

That black and white children will be hand in hand

And it started a revolution

That took us from the field

Singing those glory-filled songs

To the outhouse where we learned to pray

To the White House where we learned to continue to give God praise

Celebrate Black History 365, Not just 28 days

# Won't Take Anything for My Journey

It's a long journey,

And the road keeps rising and falling

Rising and falling


To know success

You must be acquainted with failure

A treacherous road that leads to a dead end

It snags and tears at your mind and soul

But at the end there's a story to be told

A testimony of victory

When all you've known is defeat


It's a long journey

And the road keeps rising and falling

Rising and falling

You fight in a battle

But the war is already won

Throwing blind punches,

Being crippled by gloom and the past

A past that should be buried 10,000 leagues under the sea

And lost just as the city of Atlantis


It's a long journey

And the road keeps rising and falling

Rising and falling


You long for peace

Understanding

Wisdom

Something the world cannot seem to offer

So you seek a higher power

Praying that God fills the void

When it left you out in the cold


It's a long journey

And the road keeps rising and falling

Rising and falling

But when will it all end?

# Red (Her Darkest Secret)

Crimson flowed down her thighs,

A rite of passage,

To a world that only brings,

Broken hearts,

Foggy thoughts

And years of defeat

He was deceptively perfect,

A debonair gentleman,

Burgundy roses adorned her table,

A card that read: "My love is like a red, red rose"

She hated the color red,

Reminded her of the night,

When her childhood was ripped from her arms

And womanhood began on a treacherous road

The reflection in the mirror was the girl she formerly knew

A stranger with a familiar face

She wanted to be "her" again

The innocent young girl,

That wasn't forced to give up her childhood,

To someone she called uncle, father, cousin

When showering meant only to cleanse her body,

But now it meant trying to cleanse the filthiness,

She felt possessed her soul

A soul she once felt worthy

To present to the Most High on Sunday mornings,

Now unworthy to even allow her to call upon God,

In the wee hours of the morning,

When she revealed her true emotional state

When tears poured as though Jacob's well overflowed

Crimson blood,

Burgundy roses,

She hated the color red,

It reminded her of the night,

Her childhood was stripped

And womanhood began

# Memoirs of a Daddyless Daughter

Denied in her mother's womb,

Like a bad check at Walmart,

She never knew

The man she was supposed to call father

She grew up resenting men

But giving her body to each of them

Selling her soul

For someone she called, "Daddy"

But she never knew her father

They all seemed to fill the void temporarily

Giving the false security

That her loving mother couldn't seem to give

And the man who deserted her mother

Didn't want to give

She lost her virginity

Before she knew what it meant

Had a boyfriend at the tender age of ten

And ever since

She's jumped from man to man

As if she was in a bouncer her entire life

The love of a man,

She wanted but didn't understand

Her mother tried to instill

The love and fear of God

But she ran from him,

Like a drug dealer from 5-0

Now she's calling this man 'daddy'

But she never knew her father

Who denied his own twin

For the streets and the high life

She's chasing what's missing

When he's the one she should be searching for

To tie these loose ends

# Guilty, Until Proven Innocent

Glass window shattered

As the bullet pierced the unprotected house

I know that bullet wasn't for me

My mother shattered as I fell to the floor

Blood spilling, like a well,

Unto the dusty carpeted ground

Of our two-bedroom home

On the 32nd block of MLK and Crenshaw Blvd.

Star athlete, 3.5 GPA

But your bullet didn't see that part of me

I was a number,

Another body count,

Another conversation with the brotherhood,

Of how you were trying to keep the population down

I know you didn't mean to murder me,

I wasn't your target,

But because I wore the wrong colors,

At the wrong time,

In the wrong place

You felt like, "He must be one"

You had to kill me

See, I was in unmarked Gangsta territory

Funny how no one knew but you,

How everyone knew I had a future,

But the bullet seemed to have my name

Etched across it like a wedding ring

Ready to place me into matrimony unwillingly with death

I know you want to be innocent

Told the police,

That you had an alibi

Yet at 1700 hours on that evening

Shots rang from a Chevy Malibu

Two in the front seat,

One in the back

Bumping "All Eyes on Me"

Your hands decorated in black gloves

Trigger happy

With that 9mm

And a fitted hat, hiding the guilt that played within your conscience

I know you didn't mean to murder me

And cause my mother to fall to her knees

Asking God why,

And my long-lost father to come wandering in

Because he knew his promising future was now a lie

I had plans,

That you now have the opportunity to live

And dreams

Of a justice system

That will look into the case of gang related crimes

And not let victims get lost in an abyss of numbers

And make them seem as though they don't exist,

I know you want to be innocent,

But your conscience keeps screaming "Guilty"

And in your sleep, you're chasing me,

Only for me to face you,

And you see your own reflection,

A young man,

Praying for a bright future

Guilty, until proven innocent

# I Still Have Joy

Walls around me are crashing

Yet the joy placed within me

Won't allow me to shed not one tear

Decided to face my fears head on

Almost like I'm in a crash test collision

But I'm not the dead dummy

Instead, I'm praising and giving God honor

And everyone wants my glory

But I swear they don't want half of the story

I've played David to Goliath's

Giants indeed do fall

I've had faith the size of a mustard seed

Moving mountains as high as Everest

Because my God, He's bigger

Than any situation I'll ever face

And that spirit of fear the devil is putting in my way,

God already said He gave me the spirit of power, of love, and of sound mind

So defeat is not in my vocabulary

Just the word, victory

God said, "Daughter, I'll handle it, just be still"

So Lord, I'm trusting in your divine will,

Because although I don't know where to go

Your GPS is always on time

# Confessions of a Young Christian

**Confession #1**

I came to Christ

Broken-hearted and confused

Like the Prodigal son

I had spent all I had

And with no money to give

My heart was my wealth

**Confession #2**

I'm not perfect

And although my age isn't great

My testimony is

The ashes of Black& Mild's™

The taste of Taaka™ vodka

The sounds of seconds of pleasure

Have all left my soul empty

When I thought they would fill it forever

## Confession #3

Please take me to the King

See my heart has been broken

And I know how it feels

To cry in the midnight hour

To feel as though weeping will forever endure

And morning will never come

## Confession #4

If you're looking for love

You're in the right place

Don't give your heart away

For a temporary fill

When God's love is everlasting

## Confession #5

My generation is not lost

But simply overshadowed

Overshadowed by tradition

Things that have caused us to press pause on our worship

Things that put God in a box

When He's an "out-of-the-box" God

**Confession #6**

I am beautifully and wonderfully created

I won't allow society and media

Change my ideas of what God has placed in me

So what I'm a Jesus freak?

I will let the world see

I was created for a purpose

**Confession #7**

I LOVE CHRIST!

And no I won't do it for the Vine

But I'll do anything for the True Vine

See I owe Him my life

And without Him

I wouldn't be here today to confess

That I'm just a young Christian about her Father's bid'ness

# Poetic Worship

Just in the nick of time,

You saved me,

Before the clock ran out

I mustered enough energy to shout

Faith the size of a mustard seed

No bigger than I could see

Lord help me release

The very thing that's hindering me

Tired of running in circles

Trapped in a maze

I'm tired of dead ends,

Where's the finish?

Lord, can you hear me?

I know I'm your daughter

But it's times I feel lower,

Sitting at the bottom of the Pacific

I wonder can you see me

Me.

Broken hearted

Weak

Hanging onto pain,

When you said you'd take it away

Why is it lingering here?

A fog that won't clear

I'm not trying to see too far ahead

Not looking for my fortune to be told

Lord, I just need to put off the old

And become brand new

Let You permeate

So I can be more like You

And less like me

I wanna be with You for an eternity

Eternity, how many years is that?

Infinity times infinity

Mind blown

That's how the peace you give feels

Indescribable

Incomparable

So as I sit in tears

I thank You for the years

The moments, and seconds

You've kept me here,

Despite the tears

# Queen, Be Free

Whom the Son sets free is…

Free indeed

Dear queen,

Did you know that your beauty,

Is far more precious than rubies

So no it's not your booty, but your…

Beautiful spirit, that's a sweet savor

To the Father's nostrils,

Nostradamus can't even predict

The destiny ahead of you

And I know you're wondering

Why your past keeps chasing you

Like a nightmare on Elm St.

But it's only because the enemy

Wants to see your defeat

When your name is VICTORY

Mirror, mirror on the wall

Can you help hide these flaws?

War wounds and battle scars

Like I've fought in World War II

I know how it feels

When public enemy #1 is you

Fight between the flesh and spirit

That's why Paul said we had to kill it...daily

Lord, shake me

Loose of the chains

Like Paul and Silas in the midnight hour,

Weeping may endure for a night,

But joy will come in the morning...

Light

And I know you can't see

The light at the end of the tunnel

But queen, I promise that trouble

Don't last always

Whom the Son sets free is…

Free indeed

Queen,

I know your insecurities

Have you bogged down

But God can turn it around

Can't you hear the chains

Falling from your hands and feet

Queen,

Be free

# Removing the Mask

Wearing a mask like Dunbar,

That grins and lies,

Wonder if you see the tears in my eyes,

Choking on the silent cries,

Asthmatic,

Lungs filled with the fluid of broken promises,

Childlike dreams,

I'm wishing on stars again.

Father, can you see through the mask?

You're the only one that knows my heart,

Despite all its evil devices.

I'm crying, out for you, Abba,

You're the one who adopted me,

Took me up when family forgot me,

Please stop me,

From having the nightmares of being forgotten,

You said your burden is light so I won't be downtrodden.

But this mask I wear,

Grins and doesn't tell of despair,

Daddy, do you see my tears,

Will they be dry by daybreak?

Soaring on the wings of the dawn,

Yet hidden in the secret of your tabernacle,

I know the shackles of my past,

You've set me free.

And that you were thinking of me on that Cross,

While the devil had me in a choke hold,

Ready to deliver the last punch,

Separating me from my destiny,

Even Nostradamus or the Mayans couldn't see,

Lord it's me,

And like Paul I've been fighting my flesh daily,

But I know there's no good within me,

So Father please forgive me,

And send me your grace again,

I long to be the light,

You want me to be

And I wanna be so bright,

Vegas city lights can't outshine me,

But my name I don't want them to see.

I'd rather them see you,

And be just like you,

Because I'm bound to make a mistake,

But I know you never can,

Because your ways are higher and your thoughts are deeper,

Even deeper than the Pacific Ocean

The motion of the boat during the storm,

Never caused you to be seasick or fear the present danger,

And what may be stranger

Is that the wind and waves obeyed

And if you did it then,

I know you can cause the same reaction today,

No way can I continue to sin and still call your name,

So Father from these chains,

I ask you to loose today.

Don't wanna hold the resentment,

Or the thoughts of suicide,

I'm done with homosexuality,

And I put aside my pride.

I let go of the lust,

And I promise to learn to trust,

In you with all my heart,

Because I don't want to be apart,

From you for an eternity,

All I want to hear is "servant, well done."

With you is where I wanna be.

# Define Love *(for Angie)*

What's your definition of it?

And is it easily defined?

Could you ever really explain a love so divine?

And if so, are the words in Webster?

How He encases me with His love,

Even when I deserve lesser

Lesser than what He gives,

Yet He still calls me royal,

Even though often times I'm not loyal

To Him or His son

And I pray that I let my light shine

I want it to be so bright,

I outshine Vegas city lights

And I've been putting up a fight,

With my flesh of course

Because it doesn't want me to stay the course

Or finish the race ahead

And I'm racing towards destiny

Even if the pace seems slow

See we all gotta get there,

Just maybe your track has a different flow

God I wanna be where you are

But sometimes I'm afraid to let go

And just when I feel that way

You say, "Child, it's alright"

And my hand you take

Just like a great father

Abba, is what I call you

Adopted me,

When it seems everyone forgot me

O how I praise you

And for you I let my light show

And no I'm not perfect,

But I strive to be like your Son

Who hung, bled, and died for me

And sometimes I wonder if you're ever proud of me

And I ask myself,

Am I on track with my destiny?

And there's times when I question,

The purpose you've given me

And just when I began to fall

Your love catches me

So it's obvious I can't describe

The love you have for me

Because it's indescribable,

Unconceivable,

That you love me,

And look past my flaws.

I know your hand is on me

Guiding me through these curves

So how can I describe the love,

You have just for me?

I'll simply say,

Daddy, thank you, for loving me for me!

# Hurricane

Radio silence…

This is the loudest silence I've heard

A moment where I wish screams actually haunted the space

Silence…

My thoughts are the loudest in this space

Parts of me wanting to run to the deepest pit

My heart wanting to run into your arms

I'm a wreck

Hoping that you will come and pick up the pieces

Yet they lie in wait on the floor

Almost being scattered by the wind,

The storming roaring to take me out

And you, my only shelter

But your doors have been closed

I've waited too late

My doors too closed off to accept you when you needed that same protection

Silence…

No alarms or sirens

Just dead silence as the eye of the hurricane passes

All those who were to be affected have already sheltered in place

I heeded no warnings

Just hubris in my thinking that levees wouldn't break

That tides wouldn't rise

That you'd still open your doors to me

How dare I assume such things

When I knew the storm would come

…I knew the storm would come

And things would be a mess

My regret now a dark cloud causing overcast skies

In our once sunny paradise

You always knew the storm would come

Told me to look at those clouds building in the east

I looked at you displeased

Too proud to admit that I too saw the signs

That I too saw the rain

That I too knew that an umbrella would be needed

But I'd rather trudge through mud now with flip flops

Every step growing harder and harder

I never liked this part of the clean-up process

Having to sift through a mess of debris

Love letters, broken promises, and broken heart pieces

And you, although closed off and sheltered in place

Still suffering substantial damage

Your roof leaking causing floods within the hallways of your heart

And now as I look for your doors to be open

The sign says "Under Construction"

My heart sinks

Knowing that I had ample time

But never heeding the warnings

Never looking past my own selfish ambitions

Of weathering a storm that was too big to imagine

Now your silence has thrown me

Off balance,

The air tense...

This is the loudest silence I've heard

A moment where I wish screams actually haunted this space

# We Were Royalty

Before the clinking of the chains,

The mentality of the kings and queens contained,

Before letting Willie Lynch breed those kings,

To hate those queens and leave those princes behind,

Before Martin ever had a dream,

And Malcolm ever decided that the white man was the devil,

We were kings and queens,

Negus, royalty in the highest form

God's chosen,

Even though they've tried to teach us otherwise

Wealth was already in our hands,

Yet they stripped us from our homeland

And the pattern of children being ripped from their mothers
continued

Before they stripped us from our wealth

And made us their gold mine

Before they tore down our universities

And called us uncultured swine

Before they told us Jesus was white

And that slavery was good and being brown was bad

We were the examples of light

We introduced the world to knowledge

And we spread the message of Christ

And taught everyone that He had skin like bronze and hair like wool

We held the keys to what the world could truly be

If ruling meant equality

Before Columbus sailed the ocean blue,

Revealing what those who inhabited the land already knew

Before the Transatlantic Trade stripped Mother Africa of her beloved children

Before colonization stripped us of our true identity

We were kings and queens

Crowns sitting high

We were royalty

And they've caused us to lose our identity

And take on a slave mentality

But remember this one thing

We were kings and queens.

# The Resurrector's Perspective

They say I'm guilty,

Yet no one can find fault

Just empty allegations and assumptions

They accuse without knowing

I'm the ultimate forgiver

That this was my choice

And that my voice

Has calmed seas

Caused demons to flee

Gave healing to the diseased

Yet they're displeased

With my disposition

My willingness to let them keep asking...

Are you the King of Jews?

They keep beating

And I keep bleeding

Do they even know the power in my Blood?

Dipping their dirty souls in it

Causing it to become white as snow

Sinless, blameless, faultless

All the things that I am

Yet here I am

Dying the worst death there is

Sins weighing me down

Father will this cup pass?

Did we think this plan through

I can't see You!

Father? Father? Can you hear me?

They're taking me for granted and mistreating me

Am I still your Son?

They're saying I am…

But their hearts are far from you,

Hypocrisy in the highest form

Screamed "Hosanna"

Now it's "Crucify Him"

And they don't even know

This was all in our plans

Being rejected in my own land

They don't even know

I'm love personified

Brought to life before their very eyes

Yet my flesh isn't enough for them

Miracles too much for them

Unsatisfied and displeased

Yet they can't find me guilty

Wonder if they even realized they helped me to my destiny

And I know they didn't believe me when I said

That in 3 days I'll be raised from the dead

Laughing in the face of death

Mocking the borrowed grave

Stone rolled away

Mary proclaiming to them 12 boys

132

I did as I say

They all had doubts

Thomas was just the first to speak up

Hands nail scarred, side pierced

Yet they questioned was I really real

I'm the real deal

They called me guilty

Yet I'm innocent

A lamb before the slaughter

The greatest form of love from the Father

Yet, they have allegations and assumptions

Who do you say I am?

And what will you proclaim?

# Big Mama's Reprise

Fresh greens cooking on the stove

Chicken frying in cast iron skillets

That can tell more stories than I am old

Silver hair shining

Making the sun envious of its glow

"Girl, leave that baby alone

You did the same thing"

Wisdom coming as whispers of the wind

Drawing you in with every syllable

Calming even the deepest fears

Bringing assurance only she can

Man, I miss Big Mama's voice

"Girl, you better have some sense about yourself..."

Warnings that came like a thief in the night

Snatching the essence of that secret you thought you hid

But you forgot your grandmother was a secret finder

Searching out your soul like a treasure hunter

Grabbing onto the buried treasure

Yet still giving it freedom to be

See I miss the wisdom that Big Ma would give

Her words swift, her actions swifter

Like that familiar handshake she would give

Just in the nick of time before you could even ask

I can still hear her singing down the hallway

Precious Lord, take my hand…

And I often wonder if He took her too soon

Her faith carried her through

Her prayers carrying me through

Singing soon I will be done with troubles of this world

And I often wondered if she was tired or just singing

I thought she'd live forever

An invincible character in my comic book

Forever in my heart

Immortalized in my thoughts

# Doubts

Forever is such a long time

And while hanging on to memories

I've found myself pacing and wondering

If what we had was really meant to be

You say I'm not growing

Yet

The water you're giving is laced with proteins that aren't edifying to my growth

And we seem to be stuck in the same place

Dying of thirst and starving for food

That both of us seem to be withholding from another

I'm shuddering

In this cold place

Hoping to save face and save my heart from being shattered again

Until death do us part was the promise we made

But it seems we may have twisted the timelines

Our love seems to fade

With each argument and disagreement

I was once your peace,

The calm to your raging storm

Now I seem to be the fuel that causes a hurricane of emotions

Leading us both to pain

I'm sorry I lack what you've been missing your whole life long

Am I wrong

For wanting the same peace you're longing

Tired of crying lonely tears at night

Holding my pillow tight

Waiting for you to come home

Not physically but back into the confines of my heart

It's starting to deteriorate from the lack of having been tended

I never intended

For this to go as far

But pride will make you feel as if you're the king of the world

Even if you're just a small part

And I've waited my entire life for this moment

And for love to finally find me

But it seems I've caused it to up and leave

And it's crazy

I thought I'd be more prepared

More ready to let my guard down

These iron fences so incredibly hard to penetrate

I lay awake and wonder if I'll ever be good enough to feel that love

Everyone saying it's going to be okay

But I can't help but wonder will it ever be the same again

Too many words spoken yet still left unspoken

And the arguing never ending

I'm pondering this happy ending

Asking myself if I'm worth it

Never felt worthy anyway

So I guess this last blow proves it

# Safety

Your arms were once the safest place to me,

They would welcome me,

Embrace my fears

Gently stroke my insecurities

Remind me that no matter what you'd keep me

S-A-F-E

So how is it that we've come to be

Where we are now

Barely being able to look each other in the eye

Without inhibitions creeping up within us both

When will he tire and decide to leave?

Thoughts that linger like the scent of your cologne within the depths of my mind

I wonder if you'll one day accept all the attention you've been receiving

I once knew that falling in love wouldn't actually cause me to hit the ground

Free falling without actually feeling the cold hard concrete against my back

Because I knew your arms would catch me

But now I'm reluctant to trust fall into your arms

Do you really love me or is it an illusion?

A mirage playing tricks

A cold drink in the middle of a scorching desert

Will I ever be enough for you?

I'm afraid your embrace won't feel the same

Words spoken causing damage unexplained

I can tell there are words that neither of us want to say

You were my safety net

Now I'm afraid the net is tattered

Unable to bear the weight it was meant to

The bottle is empty

No drop to satisfy my thirst for relief

I needed you

Now all I hear is insecurities when I'm with you

Whispers in the night that tell me you'll leave

That she's prettier than me

And they get louder and louder

Until they're almost screams

Choking the life out of me

And you can hardly see

I want to feel safe in your arms again

I want you to be my safety

# Saved

"IT IS FINISHED"

Three words that changed the course of time

The earth trembled in fear

Even it knew the magnitude of what had taken place

That it had lost the greatest man that would ever walk it

The G.O.A.T some may say

The sun turning to darkness

No longer wanting to shine

The true SON was shining

The veil torn

Ripped from top to bottom

No longer serving a purpose

My Savior walked from judgment hall to judgment hall

Being persecuted by men who couldn't cast the first stone

Just accusers with no premise

Six trials and they still couldn't find Him guilty

Pilate washing his hands of the matter

Before the blood could be found on him

Strange how he didn't know the Blood is what could save him

One day they screamed "Hosanna"

Laying palm branches at His feet

The next screaming "Crucify Him"

Double minded people

Stripes across His back

The weight of the cross along with the sins of humanity weighing Him down

Marching to Golgotha

Gasping for air

Feeling forsaken by His Father

Yet knowing this was the cost since He had spoken

"Let there be light"

Did they know that the darkness of their hearts still couldn't drive out His light?

The grave sealed

Death laughing

Discussing how he thought Satan had won

Grave telling them that he'll hold Him forever

They must have forgot who they were dealing with

Three days later

The tomb empty and stone rolled away

The keys to hell taken back

Mary don't weep He's no longer here

Death where is your sting?!

Grave where is your hold?!

Satan defeated forever!

Our Savior risen

Behold

He Is Alive!

And I'm glad to say that

Three words change the course of time

We're Saved

# Thought Piece #1

They don't put us in chains no more

Instead they lock us in cages

Praying we get wrapped into the slave mentality

You know,

Ya sir,

Nah sir

Please sir

Massa gone give me my check ta'morrow

Unaware that they just holding us captive

Without physically wrapping the rope around our necks

The rope now hashtags

Cleverly wrapping around brothers' and sisters' names

Seems like every week it's someone new

And were screaming SAY THEIR NAME

They screaming we're villains

Classic Batman and Joker

I get tired of mourning

Might as well wear black year around the way they killing my people

We aren't educated enough

Yet they kill us before and after we've reached potential

Dream killers in the worst way

Sandra Bland never stood a chance

Botham Jean never saw it coming

And they don't want no uprising

Not Nat Turners or Malcolm X's

Nah, they want us sweet and docile

While they continue a genocide

Some asking will it end

Gil Scott-Herron said the revolution won't be televised

He ain't never lied

# A Letter to the Man I Used to Love

I'm sorry we never made it to the "I Do's"

Fairy tale ending

House on the hills

Kids and dogs in tow

Hanging on to our every "I Love You"

Kiss before work,

Dinner and dates,

Ewwww, mommy's kissing daddy again fantasy that we'd always dreamed of

Somewhere between puberty and college

I realized that some loves are meant to be forgotten

Others tucked away in our darkest memories

Like time capsules waiting for the faithful day to be uncovered again

I'm glad you're happy...

Happy in your career and moving forth in this time

When it seems marching forward is a constant battle

I remember when you thought you couldn't make it

And I'd take you in my arms like a mother holds a weeping child

Drying tears, reassuring,

Yes, baby, I know your pain

I hope she loves you ten times better than I ever had

That she reminds you that your purpose is greater than you see

That she wraps you so tightly in love

That it swaddles away your fears

I hope she knows your fears the way I did

That she prays every morning before you rise

And every night as you shake the dust from the day's work with tired eyes

Praying that you are safe and being guided by God

I pray she never breaks your heart

That you never hear the words "it's over" from the person you've given your very being to

That she understands that you're a keeper

Not a prize but a prince

I pray you get your happily ever after

# UNTITLED #3

As I lay beside you

I wonder what would have happened

If I had dreamed of you sooner

If I had prayed for you more earnestly

If I had decided that dreams do come true

And let you love me quicker than I did

The first time I noticed your heartbeat

I noticed that both mine and yours created a dance

A rhythm I was unfamiliar with

One that frightened me at first

It hit me

Like when the bass drops in my speakers unexpectedly

Catching me off guard

I wonder if you really hear it too

The unmistakable pattern that leads me to you every time

And I be tripping

Know that you're mine

But wondering if time

Will bring about a change

And just like the wind you blow by

Or more like a tornado leaving destruction

Before you make your grand exit

Yet you calm me

And often I feel like maybe I'm trapped in a hurricane

And you are the eye and calm before the storm hits

I hit you with I miss you's and I love you's

Wanting to see if there's any inconsistency

I can't find any

And yet you love me thru it

You tell me you're true to it

And that leaving me isn't an option

And yet still

Something within me fights against the current of accepting your love

Even I am asking myself

Baby, who hurt you?

And made you a woman afraid to let a real man guard your heart

And what made you start

Doubting the blessings in your life so quickly

Wondering if Abba is listening

When He's given you every answer you long for

Why won't you just pour

Out all the pain at His feet

I'm wondering what's keeping me from being totally free

And then I look at the girl in the mirror

Not the one you see

But the soul of me that's battered and bruised

And she smiles

But it's sinister

Because she wants the free part of me to lose

And I'm tired

But the fight in me urges on

And I wanna quit,

But I've been in this too long

To just throw in the towel

God keeps throwing it back

Saying "Daughter I got you"

I heard them asking "Who's child is that?"

And rightfully they don't wanna say

Think I've lost my mind, crazy

But I'd rather put my faith into something I can't see

Than continuously be disappointed by what's in front of me

As I lay beside you

And I wonder what would have happened

If I dreamed of you sooner

If I prayed more earnestly

If I decided dreams do come true

Would it be more believable

That God blessed me with you.

# Tugging At Heaven

Another space,

Another time,

Another moment...

I once found purpose in making others happy

Seeing the smile on their faces would brighten mine

To the point where I'd happily mistake it for my own

But remind me, where exactly is mine?

And what happened to joy everlasting?

And what happened to self-love and acceptance?

Not necessarily being complacent but content.

Paul said I glory in my trials

But what happens when the trials blind what's ahead

And I think I've been around this mountain 100 times before

Children of Israel syndrome

When will I learn...?

And when will I look in the mirror and be truly happy with the image staring at me?

Guess Mulan had the same complex...

Mirror mirror on the wall,

What's with all the flaws?

I don't need them to do a disappearing acting like Houdini

More like embrace them, like Jesus...

And I get it,

He's accepting,

But why can't I accept me?

I wanna stop trying to figure it out,

But reason says there has to be a reason for everything

Cause and effect one might say

So what's the cause of me feeling unworthy today?

Is it the sin I committed last year,

Or the one that happened just moments ago

When I cursed my own self and asked God why me

And I know I have no business questioning my purpose

But I've been blinded by a world that says

To be Christian you gotta be perfect

And why can't I just let this process be

Instead of pressing reset every time something happens that ain't pleasing

See that's the reason I'm in this place now

I see why Moses got frustrated with the Israelites

Comfortability kills

And I don't wanna be caught with a vessel full of treasure

Talking about Lord I buried because I thought it'd bring you joy still

What a sad state when He calls my name

Asking why I never trusted Him and still proclaimed His name

And I don't want my work to be in vain,

But I gotta be real with myself,

The path I'm on, I'm afraid

To see how it'll all end if I don't get my heart right

And Lord I know you're the only one that sees all its evil devices

And the enemy been whispering foul things

And so far, I've been believing them,

But I'm not trying to die and lose my soul for an eternity with him

And some days I'm not gone lie,

I question why you put this thorn in my side

And every time I think I'm better,

It sticks me harder each time

And see that devil smooth,

He swears the pain will leave if I pull it

But I know you're building me tough,

So I can fight battles with ease

And I know you see every tear

And I know you'll wipe them all away,

There's just one problem Lord

Some days I wish you could hug me

And I feel you tugging on me

Thanks for being the best Father a girl could have

Your love is everlasting,

Just wish I could always see that

And I know I'm not a failure in your eyes

Just wish I always believed that

And I know you made me beautiful in your sight

But I wish the mirror always reflected that

And I wish I didn't reject the fact

That you made me with purpose way before I was conceived,

Glad you gave Jeremiah the inspiration to write that,

I need it most days

And I need you more than I really can explain,

Some days my desire is deeper than others

But right now I need to hear you say

That I'm loved and you got me

That it'll all work out in time

That I'm not alone and you know

Sometimes my tears aren't always pain

And I know I gotta get my faith up

Start trusting you forreal

And Lord I'm really trying I promise I am

Just some days are harder still

And I'm just hoping and praying

That this season isn't in vain,

That going through this valley one last time,

Won't make me give up

And I should've gotten this lesson God,

A long time ago

I'm sorry it's taken so long,

But I just want you to know,

That I love you more than anything

And that all I want is you

Just lead me in a plain path

And continue to guide my way

And hide me in your tabernacle

Your place of safety I long to rest

God, I need you now, forevermore

Just don't let me fail this test

# Validation

Validation

A silent killer

An addiction many don't realize they have

Sneaking up on them

Needle straight to the heart

Feeding false securities,

Fallacies, dreams

What's validation anyway?

Webster defines it as

The act of recognizing or illustrating the worthiness of something,

Ah, worth...

So many walking around

Feeling as though they aren't worth the time

Worth the effort

Worth the love

Not realizing there's one person

Who felt they were enough

And we're all guilty of it

Not feeling worthy enough

Looking for that drug to fill our veins

But highs are temporary

And lows feel lower

When you come off the high of temporary sanity

Instead of searching for true peace

Some might as well be dope dealers

The way they feeding lies

Telling people they approve

Then when asked, they deny

Some might as well be dope dealers

They selling false validation

Like an 80s crack pusher

Not caring of the destruction

Self-gain is all they see

True to the game

They'll go years

Selling to fiends

And we keep buying it

Thinking that it'll change

But if she didn't love me then

What makes me think it'll be different

And if she thought only of herself ten years ago

What makes me think she cares now

She worse than the rest of them

But family supposed to have your back somehow

One thing about addiction

It can tear you from those who genuinely love

Leaving you high and dry on the streets

Asking yourself why they said goodbye

Withdrawal ain't no joke,

Getting clean is harder each time

But when you start to see things slip away

Do you choose to keep running back

Or face reality this time

And if she didn't love you then,

What makes you think it'll be different,

If she didn't love me then

What makes me think it'll be different...

Validation made me keep running back

To the very person that hurt me

# Rhythm of Letting Go

My first love was like a sweet melody

I'd love to hear it played constantly

Soothing to my ears

Each time something different caught my attention

Eventually, the record started skipping

The once calming trance became haunting

I began to recognize all the flaws with it

The rhythm was off

The pitch was distorted

Nothing sounded the same

So instead of throwing just the record away

I threw away the entire record player

What good was it

If it was going to make my favorite song skip?

Years passed and other records came and went

Until one day I realized

It quite possibly was the record.

But why would I trash it

After all, it was my favorite

And even though others had claimed it as their own

It was still close to my heart

One day another melody began to play

Catching my attention ever so suddenly,

Sneakily one might say

Playing over and over until I caught the rhythm

And I couldn't put it down

Forgot about that old record

It was worn out anyhow

The new melody made me forget the flaws of the old

And while it had a few scratches

It never skipped like the old one did

It never let me down

# Cover Me

Like the warmest blanket

On the coldest winter night

Cover me

You remind me that even in fear

That beauty can blossom

Your love reminds me

That broken things can be loved too

You cover me

Even on the days

When I'd rather be left in the cold

Sulking in my own tears

And wondering if I was ever good enough to be loved

You assure me that even beauty can be seen through ashes

And I so graciously rise like a phoenix into your arms

You cover me

On days when my blanket doesn't suffice

It has a few holes

Broken-heartedness I dare not hold on to

Yet I haven't found time to patch them up

Yet you cover it with your own warmth

And remind me that time mends everything

Even the deepest wounds and cuts

And I faintly smile

Shedding tears

Praying that you never fade away

And that the fairy tale has a happy ending

And that I never awake from this blessed dream

You cover me

But it is I who wants to cover you

Give you the same thing

As you've given me

Love you beyond what you've seen

I want to cover the scars

Left on your heart

From lovers who never understood your worth

They began missing their water when the well went dry

Or better yet missing the warmth

When the blanket was torn into shreds

By their own self sabotage

I cover you

You cover me

God covers us

Love covers we

# The Cost of Love

First let me say I apologize,

I find that in this society

Many care nothing of their actions

Or how they affect everyone

So let me be the first to say

I apologize

I apologize for holding on too tight

Like a scared toddler at night

Holding for dear life

On to that sacred teddy bear

Hoping that its warmth would save him

From whatever monsters lurk within the darkness of his room

It seems I should've let you go years ago,

I've long since passed those toddler years

Yet my very being still yearns to hold on to you

I apologize for loving too hard

Seems maybe I took it too far

When the Father said strive to love as Christ

Who can love someone so unconditionally anyway

When they've caused them to bleed

But it seems the wounds don't hurt as much

At least not as bad as loving you thru a thick glass

Of unspoken sayings that's caused our separation

But who allows love to separate them

And I apologize if I didn't love you enough

It seems as if I were the one who fell short

And you were the only victim of my shortcomings,

I apologize that I could never quite

Pull it together and love you like you wanted

Seems the tight grip you had on my heart

Was not a hug at all

But suddenly the grips of a python,

Waiting to crush whatever love I had left for you

Crazy, you still couldn't squeeze tight enough

I apologize that I still love you

Despite your attempts to let me go

I still hold tight like that toddler

Love hard as I was shown

And fighting more for us than you ever will.

And maybe I'm trippin' because I just don't wanna lose you

Not understanding

I've already lost

# About the Author

Jasmine *"J Nicole"* Macklin, a native of Jackson, MS, discovered her passion for music and poetry at a young age, nurtured by her education and church roots. She began singing in church and went on to perform in school choirs and ensembles, most notably leading Total Praize, the student-led gospel ensemble at the Mississippi School of the Arts. Under her leadership, the group performed background vocals for Sherry Pruitt and Jeff Stone. She later served as a member, section leader, and student director for the renowned Tougaloo College Concert Choir.

A versatile creative, J Nicole is both a songwriter and composer. She released her debut single, "FaithWalk", in 2022 and is currently working on her first EP, Journey 2 Destiny. Blending gospel, R&B, hip-hop, and soul, her sound defies traditional gospel labels while maintaining authenticity.

Poetry has been a lifelong form of expression for J Nicole, beginning in her teenage years as a means of coping and connection. She began performing spoken word during her time at the Mississippi School of the Arts and Tougaloo College, releasing her debut spoken word single, "Transparency, Pt. 1", in 2023. *Confessions of a Young Poet* is her first book release.

Beyond her artistry, J Nicole is a devoted wife to Thaddeus and mother to Jeremiah. She serves faithfully at HOPE City Church and enjoys other creative pursuits, including graphic design and drawing.

www.ingramcontent.com/pod-product-compliance
Lightning Source LLC
Chambersburg PA
CBHW031524120626
46545CB00005B/1988